MARANATHA

topics on Christian meditation

Decio Martins de Medeiros
São Paulo – Brasil – 2021

Maranatha

This is a translation of the original in Portuguese: Maranata.

Bibliographic Information:
Author: Decio Martins de Medeiros.
Title: Maranatha.
Subtitle: topics on Christian meditation.
Location, Year: São Paulo-Brasil, 2024.
Pages: 65 pages 6"x9" size.
Subject: 1.Meditation

Maranatha

Table of Contents

Maranatha

Maranatha

The expression Maranatha appears in the Christian Bible in 1 Corinthians 16:22.

In searching for the origin of the expression Maranatha, we find that the Aramaic word "Marãn" means "Our Lord will come." The Aramaic word "Athá" following Marãn means "Christ is here and will return."

If this expression is read as 'Maran-atha', it means 'our Lord has come' or 'our Lord is coming'.

If the expression Maranatha is read as 'Marana-tha', it means 'come, our Lord', which echoes the call 'Come, Lord Jesus' found in Revelation 22:20.

Maranatha

The word Maranatha is a prayer-word used as a mantra by members of the World Community for Christian Meditation. [1]

---

[1] The website of the World Community for Christian Meditation is https://wccm.org/

Christian Faith

Christ is the Divine Son incarnate. Christ has a human mother and a divine Father. Christ is the perfect union of humanity with divinity.

We can relate to Christ in both dimensions: as disciples of Christ, our human teacher, and with the inner Christ, since we are temples of His Divine Spirit.[2]

Christ is our Master and Lord.[3]

C.S. Lewis said: *"I am trying to prevent anyone from saying the ridiculous thing that people say about Him: 'I'm willing to accept Jesus as a great moral teacher, but I don't accept His claim to be God.' That is the one thing we must not say. A man who was merely*

---

[2] 1Corinthians 6,19
[3] John 13,13

a man and said the sort of things Jesus said would not be a great moral teacher. He would either be a lunatic – on the level with a man who says he is a poached egg – or else he would be the Devil of Hell. You must make your choice. Either this man was, and is, the Son of God, or else a madman or something worse. You can shut Him up for a fool, you can spit at Him and kill Him as a demon; or you can fall at His feet and call Him Lord and God. But let us not come with any patronizing nonsense about His being just a great human teacher. He has not left that open to us. He did not intend to." [4]

---

[4] Book *Mere Christianity* by C.S. Lewis.

And the other beliefs?

Regarding the question of following the truth of other religions or following Jesus Christ, Simone Weil said: *"Christ likes that we prefer the truth to him because, being Christ, he is the truth. If someone leaves him to pursue the truth, that person will not go very far before falling into his arms."* [5]

---

[5] page 27 of book Waiting for God, by Simone Weil.

A Christian Tradition

The apostle Paul recommended praying regularly.[6]

Subsequently, John Cassian, born around the year 360, rethought, experimented with, and systematized in his "Conferences" the teachings he received from the early Christian monks, the "Desert Fathers."

In Conference 9, titled "First Conference of Abbot Isaac," in chapter 25, John Cassian speaks of a more sublime form of prayer than the Lord's Prayer:

"Although this prayer [the Lord's Prayer] seems to contain all the fullness of perfection, since it was given by the Lord, there is a prayer that leads them to a higher stage, a

---

[6] 1 Thessalonians 5,17

fervent prayer experienced by few. This prayer transcends all human thoughts and is not distinguished by any sound of the voice, any movement of the tongue, or expression of words. The mind, enlightened by the infusion of celestial light, is not described by human language but flows richly like from an abundant spring in an accumulation of thoughts, and ineffably addresses God, expressing in the smallest amount of time things so great that the mind, when it returns to its normal state, cannot express". [7]

Chapters 35 and 36 bring us the following teachings on how to practice silent prayer: We turn to our heart, close the door, and pray to our Father who is in Heaven. Completely distance our heart from the tumult and noise of thoughts and worries. In secret intimacy, manifest to the Lord our silent prayer. With a

____

[7] The Conferences of John Cassian, Christian Classics Ehtereal Library https://www.ccel.org/ccel/cassian/conferences.html

heart open to God but closed to the outside world, with lips sealed and in deep silence, we beseech the Lord, who searches the hearts. Only with the heart and soul attentive do we present our supplications solely to God. Observe the deepest silence. Our prayer should be frequent.

The Benedictine monks John Main and Laurence Freeman have worldwide propagated this monastic tradition of silent prayer called Christian Meditation.

The 'formula' presented by John Main[8] is: "...prayer is not a matter of talking to God, but of listening to Him, or being with Him. ...if we want to pray and listen, we must remain quiet and calm, reciting a short verse numerous times. Sit comfortably and relax. Make sure you are sitting upright. Breathe calmly and harmoniously. Close your eyes and then, in

---

[8] Word into Silence, John Main, Londres: Darton,Longman and Todd,1980, pp.10-1.

your mind and heart, begin to repeat the word you have chosen as your meditation word. Some of these words have been used as mantras for Christian meditation by the early Church. One of them is the word 'maranatha.' This is the mantra I recommend to most beginners, the Aramaic phrase 'maranatha', which means 'Come, Lord. Come, Lord Jesus.'"

Contemplation

Contemplation is the forgetting of oneself, remaining in a state of complete intellectual emptiness, open and exposed to the love of God.

An analogy is sunbathing. We make no effort, we offer no resistance to the sunlight. We simply expose ourselves to the sun.

In Christian meditation, we make no effort, forget ourselves, offer no resistance, and simply expose ourselves to the Holy Spirit. May He come and fill our hearts, our core, our inner being.

Maranatha <come, Lord>, we are the temple of the Holy Spirit.[9]

---

[9] 1Corínthians 6,19

According to the Catechism of the Catholic Church (CCC):

"Christian tradition comprises three types: vocal prayer, meditation, and contemplation" [10]

One should not confuse meditation on a topic with silent prayer, or centering prayer, which we refer to here as Christian meditation.

Meditation on a topic uses thought, imagination, emotion, and desire, and confronts the considered topic with the reality of our lives. [11]

Contemplation, silent prayer, centering prayer is the simple expression of the mystery of prayer. It is a silent love. [12]

---

[10] CCC 2721
[11] CCC 2723
[12] CCC 2724

"*The choice of time and duration for contemplation depends on a determined will, revealing the secrets of the heart. One does not contemplate when one has time; rather, time is arranged to be with the Lord, with the firm determination not to withdraw it during the journey, regardless of the trials and the dryness of the encounter. One cannot always meditate; but one can always enter into contemplation, regardless of health conditions, work, or affectivity. The heart is the place of seeking and meeting, in poverty and faith.*" [13]

'*Contemplation is the prayer of the child of God, the forgiven sinner who consents to receive the love with which they are loved and wishes to respond by loving even more. But they know that their responsive love is what the Holy Spirit pours into their heart because everything is a grace from God. Contemplation is the humble and poor surrender to the loving*

---

[13] CCC 2710

will of the Father, in ever-deepening union with His beloved Son.' [14]

'Thus, contemplation is the simplest expression of the mystery of prayer. It is a gift, a grace; it can only be received in humility and poverty. It is a covenant relationship established by God in the depths of our being. Contemplation is communion: in it, the Holy Trinity conforms man, the image of God, 'to His likeness.'' [15]

"Contemplation is also, par excellence, the powerful time of prayer. In it, the Father fills us with strength through the Holy Spirit so that our inner being may be strengthened, Christ may dwell in our hearts through faith, and we may be rooted and grounded in love." [16]

---

[14] CCC 2712
[15] CCC 2713
[16] CCC 2714

'Contemplation is silence, this 'symbol of the world to come' or 'silent language of love.' In contemplation, words are not discourses but kindling that feeds the fire of love. It is in this silence, unbearable to the 'outer' man, that the Father reveals to us His incarnate, suffering, dead, and resurrected Word, and that the filial Spirit makes us participate in Jesus' prayer.'[17]

---

[17] CCC 2717

Heart-core-center

As the Brazilian religious song says: *"Open wide the doors of your heart and let the light of heaven in."*

In the context of spiritual matters, when we use the word 'heart,' we are not referring to the circulatory organ, which in English is 'heart.' In spirituality, when we use the word 'heart,' we are referring to the core, the innermost part of a person. In English, for the heart as a core, the word 'core' is used.

A human person is both a bodily and spiritual being. The human person is spiritual because their body is animated by a spiritual principle of life called the soul. The human body (material) united with the human soul (spiritual) forms one single human nature. The soul is created by God at the exact moment of human conception. The integral person (body and soul) comes into being at the moment of conception by the biological parents.

The individual human being is a substantial unity with various dimensions: emotional, psychic, historical, social, cosmic, material, etc. What happens to the individual human being impacts all of these dimensions.

The human being exists only in their entirety; that is, one element without the others does not represent the integral human being. Our entire being—our intellect, will, emotions, and intuition—are all involved in our knowledge of God. God does not relate to the human being in fragmented terms, but the whole person is important to God.

The components of the human being according to Witness Lee[18] are three: body +

---

[18]   https://www.barnesandnoble.com/w/the-economy-of-god-witness-lee/1129293507

soul + spirit. The three parts of the soul are: mind + will + emotion. The three parts of the spirit are conscience + intuition + fellowship. The four parts of the heart are the three parts of the soul + conscience. The Bible views the person from a holistic perspective, although in certain passages it uses other elements to represent the person. Sometimes it uses the term soul to refer to the whole person, sometimes it emphasizes the material aspect (body) and/or the immaterial aspect (soul or spirit); other times it highlights other aspects (heart; strength; mind; intelligence; etc.).

For meditation, the body and mind need to be completely relaxed, so that the spirit can be fully open and receptive to the Divine Spirit. Brother Angelino, in his prayer before Christian meditation, asks that the Holy Spirit of God relax the body, calm the mind, and soothe the heart.

According to Bede Griffiths[19], the mantra serves to restore the soul, bringing it back to its center, and uniting the entirety of the person (body, soul, and spirit) with the Divine Spirit.

The human spirit is the point of transcendence of the self. At this point, body and soul go beyond their human limitations, opening up to the infinite, the eternal, the divine.

Meditation is the passage beyond the body and soul to that point of the spirit.

The goal of meditation is to center the body and soul in the depths of the spirit, where the human spirit meets the Divine Spirit.

It is interesting that the word "spirit" is sometimes used in the New Testament to refer to the human and other times to the divine: because it is the meeting point.

---

[19] "The Function of the Mantra," a lecture by Bede Griffiths.

The spirit is the refined point of the soul. It is the point of self-transcendence, from which we go beyond ourselves and receive the Divine Spirit into our hearts, that is, into the center of our being. The repetition of the mantra is a simple way to keep all the faculties of the soul and body centered on this point of the spirit.

For the Christian, the point of the spirit is the point where the love of God floods the heart through the Holy Spirit.

As Laurence Freeman[20] explains, John Main's view is that the primary purpose of the silence of meditation is to allow us to find our own spirit. As we become quieter, we also become more aware of what the spirit is, as we awaken more consciously to the dimension of our being.

We understand that the spirit exists in a dimension that differs from both the mind and

---

[20] "The Light That Comes from Within" by Laurence Freeman.

the body, that the spirit is not exactly within the body, like a ghost in a machine, nor exactly in the mind; although it is above space, it is more like a mysterious point where body and mind unite and transcend in their activity or process.

As we progress on the journey of meditation, we realize, over time, that we cannot make and establish definitive oppositions between these three dimensions (body, mind, and spirit), for through the discovery of the spirit, we become more grounded, more real in the other two dimensions as well. Thus, the function of meditation is to learn to be.

The function of the silence of meditation is to allow consciousness to naturally travel back to its exact starting point. This point is the center of our being, where we find ourselves close to God, where we come into harmony with ourselves and with the Divine Spirit.

Silence and Solitude

Henri J. M. Nouwen teaches us[21] that the spiritual life is a gift from the Holy Spirit. However, this does not mean that we should wait passively until the gift is offered.

We find ourselves surrounded by so much internal and external noise that it becomes difficult to hear God.

True prayer is being all ears for God. The essence of prayer is listening, placing oneself in the presence of God.

Without silence, without solitude, it is impossible to lead a spiritual life. Silence and solitude begin when there is time and space for God, and for Him alone.

---

[21] Making All Things New, by Henri J. M. Nowen.

Christ said: *"But when you pray, go into your room, close the door and pray to your Father, who is unseen."* [22]

We should start by planning for a little silence, some solitude, a few minutes each day, to pay attention to the voice of God within us.

As we empty ourselves of our worries, we discover with our minds and hearts that we have never been alone, that the Divine Spirit is with us all the time.

Little by little, we learn to hear God's gentle voice.

But what about the countless distractions? We should not fight these distractions, nor give them our attention. We must let them pass.

---

[22] Matthew 6,6

When we realize we've been distracted, we should return to the mantra. The mantra 'Maranatha' helps us focus our attention on the presence of God. The mantra 'Maranatha' serves as a point of return whenever we stray.

By setting aside time and space for God, our hearts become like silent cells where the Divine Spirit can dwell.

Henri Nouwen[23] teaches that:

"Solitude is, therefore, a space of purification and transformation, of the great battle and the great encounter. It is not merely a means to an end, it is an end in itself, the space where Christ reshapes us into His image and frees us from the world's victimizing compulsions; it is the space of our salvation.

Silence complements and intensifies solitude. Silence is the means to make solitude a reality. Silence is an indispensable discipline for

---

[23] "The Way of the Heart", by Henri Nouwen

the spiritual life. Silence is solitude practiced in action.

Silence makes us pilgrims. Pilgrimage means that one must control their tongue. ... Speaking involves us in worldly matters, and it is very difficult to be involved without being entangled by the world and corrupted by it.

Silence guards the inner fire. This warmth is the life of the Holy Spirit within us. Thus, silence is the discipline by which the inner fire of God is tended and kept alive.

Silence teaches us how to speak. A word with power is one that comes from silence, one that bears fruit is the one that emerges from silence and returns to it."

The word Maranatha repeated in our minds "in a discreet and persistent way, so that it becomes like a fence around a garden where the shepherding of God can be sensed. What might initially seem like nothing more than an interesting metaphor slowly descends from the mind to the heart. There, it can offer the context in which an inner transformation, by *the Father who transcends all words and human concepts, is able to take place." In this way, the word Maranatha leads "to the quiet pastures where we can dwell in His loving presence. This meditative preaching is a means of practicing the ministry of silence."*

"The Desert Fathers did not think of solitude as merely being alone, but as being with God. They did not think of silence as synonymous with not speaking, but with listening to Him; both are the context in which prayer is practiced."

"To pray is to descend, with the mind, into the heart, and there to place oneself before the omnipresent and omniscient face of the Lord within. Silent prayer is sustained by the presence of God with the mind in the heart, that is: in that point of our being where there are no divisions or distinctions, where we are one. There, the Spirit of God dwells, and the great encounter takes place. There heart speaks to heart, for we are in the presence of the Lord's omniscient face within us."

The person engages in Christian meditation in silence, with eyes closed, sitting with an upright spine, body relaxed yet alert, mind calm, heart peaceful, slowly repeating in the mind a Christian word or phrase, such as the Aramaic word 'Maranatha,' which means 'Come, Lord.'

Breathing should be calm. Do not think or imagine anything. If thoughts and images come to mind, they should be regarded as distractions, and one should humbly return to the repetition of the word.

Christian Meditation is also called Silent Prayer, Contemplative Prayer, or Prayer of the Heart.

Always Alert

When we are awake, we occupy ourselves with the activities of the present, and, as a side effect, also worry about the future or think about the past.

When we are asleep, we are resting, recharging our batteries, and recovering.

When we are meditating, we are taking care of our spiritual health, open to our divine and hidden friend, the Holy Spirit.

Each one of us is a unique creation of God. We are all different. Some people find it easy to fall asleep, while others do not. Some people find it easy to begin meditating, while others do not. There are techniques that can help with both sleeping and meditating.

Relaxation techniques, such as the method of relaxing each part of your body, from head to toe, help induce sleep, and these same techniques also prepare us for meditation. To sleep, we need to be relaxed. To meditate, we need to be relaxed and focused.

After relaxing, to fall asleep, close your eyes, feel that you are alone in a dark room, and don't think, don't think, don't think...

After relaxing, if you wish to meditate, begin to pray to the divine and hidden friend who dwells within your heart, and ask Him for the grace to be still, to surrender to His care, and to open yourself to His love.

After relaxing your body, calm your mind and soothe your heart, using your senses to bring yourself back to the present moment, letting go of thoughts about the past and stopping any worries about the future.

Focus, stay alert, vigilant, with full attention, while mentally repeating your mantra: Maranatha.

Anthony de Mello wrote a book titled 'Awareness'.

The English word 'awareness' comes from 'aware', which means to have knowledge or perception of something. It can be translated as being conscious, being attentive, being vigilant, being aware of everything happening around you.

I think awareness is a little door that a person opens from within. It is important to be conscious, to awaken the Ego in relation to the illusions about the Self.

Consciousness is understanding that what you call the Self is nothing more than the sum of your past experiences, your conditioning, your programming. The Self is not your thoughts, your body, your name, your career, your beliefs, or your religion. The Self is not your labels. Labels belong to the Ego. What constantly changes is the Ego. The Self does not always change. The Self is the observer.

Self-observation is watching everything within you and around you, as distantly as possible, as if you were another person. Face things as if you had no connection to them. Be a passive observer, don't interfere, watch, observe, don't try to change anything, don't judge, don't take action. End the story of good and evil, end all judgments, just observe.

To be aware of reality is to observe, see things, discard illusions, fantasies, and begin to connect with the facts.

When you understand what the Self is, nothing will hurt you, because no one can reach your Self, only your Ego can be affected.

When anxiety comes, don't fight it, just observe it and let it pass.

To disconnect from your Ego, observe everything as if it were happening to someone else: without comments, without judgment, without interference, without trying to change anything, just understanding.

Stay conscious, try to be both a participant and an observer.

Consciousness is not concentration. Concentration is focus. Consciousness is being open to anything that enters your field of awareness.

Your essential Self is not your profession, your clothes, or your name. The Ego is all your labels.

Be aware of the reality around you. Awareness means observing; observing what is happening inside you and around you. Look, observe, spend hours watching people, trees, birds, stones, and grass. See the reality that lies beyond words and concepts. Give up your concepts, give up your opinions, give up your prejudices, give up your judgments.

When you turn on the light of awareness, the darkness disappears.

According to an Eastern saying: *"If the eye is unobstructed, the result is vision; if the ear is unobstructed, the result is hearing; if the nose is unobstructed, the result is smell; if the mouth is unobstructed, the result is taste; if the mind is unobstructed, the result is wisdom."*

Preparation for Christian Meditation

Brother Angelino taught us to pray to the Holy Spirit before beginning the Christian meditation session:

"In the name of the Father, the Son, and the Holy Spirit. O Divine and hidden Friend. I feel that I often fail in prayer and in life, but I rejoice in knowing that deep within me, You pray incessantly to the Father. Grant me the grace at this hour to be still, surrendered to Your care, open to Your love, and thus be led by Your ways. Relax my body, calm my mind, soothe my heart, so that You may work in them as You wish. Amen."

The Now, the Present

Our senses pick up stimuli from both the external world and the inner world.

In our daily lives, our senses are more attuned to the external world.

When we sit to meditate, pray, or contemplate, it's helpful to direct our senses inward.

"But you, when you pray, go into your room, close the door, and pray to your Father, who is in secret..."[24]

The Now, the Present, is what we experience with our senses in a state of alertness and wakefulness.

---

[24] Matthew 6,6

Maranatha

How do we direct our senses to the inner world?

By making sensory contact with internal events: what I feel inside me, muscle tensions, movements, bodily sensations.

<u>Sight</u>: Close the eyelids to block out the external world and focus the eyes on an internal point.

<u>Hearing</u>: Shift attention from external sounds to internal sounds, such as the "sound" of the mantra repeated mentally: Ma-ra-na-tha, Ma-ra-na-tha...

<u>Touch</u>: Stop moving and pay attention to bodily sensations: itching, pressure from the chair on the body.

<u>Smell</u>: Extend the acts of inhaling and exhaling.

Taste: Pay attention to sensations on the roof of the mouth. Notice the taste we feel in the mouth.

Try it. Use your senses to feel the now, to experience the present moment: listen to the sounds around you and the internal sounds. Pay attention to bodily sensations. Observe your breath, feel the airflow. Just observe, and don't let other thoughts intrude.

Repetition of the Christian Word

Laurence Freeman says: "Abbot Isaac teaches that the repetition of the word (mantra, or sacred phrase) leads to poverty of spirit, the first of the beatitudes, the foundation of all happiness. It leads us to poverty because we abandon all the wealth of imagination and thoughts." ..."Obviously, the mantra constitutes discipline, it is not an end in itself. It is a path to poverty of spirit; it is not the Kingdom itself."[25]

We believe that in Christian meditation, as contemplative prayer, we seek the "pearl of great value," letting go of all thoughts so that the Holy Spirit can work in us. "The Kingdom of Heaven is also like a merchant seeking fine pearls. When he finds one of great value, he

---

[25] Os olhos do coração, by Laurence Freeman, published in Brazil by Palas Atenas, 2004.

goes, sells all his possessions, and buys that pearl."[26]

---

[26] Matthew 13,45-46

Breathing

Breathe in sync with the syllables of the mantra Ma-ra-na-tha, which you silently repeat in your mind, not aloud.

Inhale with the syllable Ma.
Exhale with the syllable ra.
Inhale with the syllable na.
Exhale with the syllable tha.

The ideal breathing rhythm for relaxation is about 4 seconds per syllable.

Emptying Oneself

Here are some points about what I've read regarding "poverty of spirit" and how to practice it through Christian meditation, a simple but not easy formula.

Christ taught that "Blessed are the poor in spirit, for theirs is the Kingdom of Heaven."[27]

Laurence Freeman explains: "...what Jesus called poverty of spirit... is exactly what we develop through the practice of meditation. It doesn't mean that I have nothing or that I don't appreciate anything. It means appreciating freely what one has, without the fear of losing it and, therefore, without a tendency toward violence. It is a very difficult state to develop, being detached from the people we love,

____

[27] Matthew 5,3

allowing them to be themselves. However, according to Jesus, this is the first condition for human happiness."[28]

Regarding the Bible story where the rich man asks Jesus what he needs to do to inherit the Kingdom of God,[29] I understand from Laurence Freeman's teachings that the rich man should empty himself in spirit to allow the action of the Holy Spirit, which is the way to be touched by God. Meditation is this: focusing on the repetition of the mantra (Maranatha, or another), letting all thoughts pass, that is, leaving the spirit poor of thoughts, allowing the Holy Spirit to fill your temple, which is the human body.[30]

A person 'full of themselves' has no space in their heart to host the Holy Spirit.

---

[28] Os olhos do coração, by Laurence Freeman, published in Brazil by Palas Atenas, 2004.

[29] Matthew 19,16-26; Mark 10,17-27; Luke 18,18-27

[30] 1Corinthians 6,19

So, in Christian meditation, a person empties their Ego to make room to be in the presence of the divine.

The person, in vigilance, present in their true Self, exposes themselves to the light of the Divine Spirit's presence.

Presence with presence.

Fruits of Christian Meditation

Regarding the fruits of Christian meditation, Laurence Freeman explains during the retreats he leads that they do not occur during the meditation session itself.

If you experience any visual or sensory impressions during meditation, you should let them pass and not be concerned with them.

The fruits of meditation will come over time and will be perceived by the people with whom you have relationships.

Besides harmonizing the dimensions of your being, you receive the fruits of the Holy Spirit: love, joy, peace, patience, kindness, goodness, faithfulness, gentleness, and self-control.[31]

---

[31] Galatians 5,22

The World Community for Christian Meditation teaches that Christian meditation is about *"becoming the person God needs us to be, through the integration of the wisdom of our deepest self with the capacities of our ego. By silencing the daily thoughts of our superficial self and focusing our attention on God, we open ourselves to the work that God's love is doing at the center of our being. Our word/prayer, 'Maranatha,' then becomes a powerful call of love. The effects of this, the response to it, are a wholly transformative life experience: we become aware of the spiritual dimension, and this experience, in turn, adds a contemplative dimension to our way of being and living. We find the best way to describe the effects of this and the qualities it produces in us in the words of St. Paul in Galatians 5,22: love, joy, peace, patience, kindness, goodness, faithfulness, gentleness, and self-control. These are not qualities that we can obtain through our own efforts in our daily lives, but they are signs of what God has already accomplished in us."* [32]

Meditation Sessions

It is recommended to practice Christian meditation daily for 20 minutes in the morning and 20 minutes in the late afternoon.

Weekly sessions with other meditators are also recommended.

A suggested schedule for the weekly Christian meditation session might be:

7:00 PM - Reading about Christian Meditation, with texts by John Main, Laurence Freeman, or another Christian author, to reinforce the following characteristic points of Christian Meditation: Christian Meditation takes place in the heart, not in the mind. In Christian Meditation, we aim to dismiss the noise of the mind, but not with great effort; instead, with a letting go and letting come. Christian

Meditation requires attention, which is a state of alertness, not sleep. In Christian Meditation, we use a Christian word as a mantra but do not use images or other resources.

7:20 PM - Prayer of preparation for Christian Meditation, written by brother Angelino Feitosa: In the name of the Father, the Son, and the Holy Spirit. O Divine and hidden friend. I feel that I often fail in prayer and in life, but I rejoice in knowing that deep within me, you pray without ceasing to the Father. Grant me the grace at this hour to be still, entrusted to your care, open to your love, and thus be led by your ways. Relax my body, calm my mind, and soothe my heart so that you may work in them as you wish. Amen.

7:21 PM - Sit with your back straight, body relaxed, heart calm, and mind attentive to a Christian word. The suggested mantra is Maranatha, a Hebrew word meaning "Come, Lord."

*30 seconds of silence, ring the bell.

*20 minutes of silence where you allow your heart to be exposed to the Divine Holy Spirit, and your mind repeats the mantra until the bell rings.

7:40 PM - Reading of the Gospel for the upcoming Sunday.

7:45 PM - Comments on the Gospel.

8:00 PM - Final prayers.

Sunbath for the Body and the Soul

There are many activities a person needs to perform in their daily life.

It's important to take care of physical health with healthy eating, physical activity, rest, sleep, and annual check-ups.

It's important to care for emotional health by feeling useful through work, whether paid or not, positive thinking, stress management, and self-image.

It's important to manage financial health with weekly monitoring.

It's important to maintain social health with healthy relationships, listening and being heard, giving and receiving.

It's important to look after mental health with studies, research, reading, writing, games, and mental exercises.

It's important to attend to spiritual health with regular prayers, both vocal and silent, biblical readings and studies, weekly mass participation to nourish oneself with the Word and the bread that came down from Heaven, connection with nature, practice of silence, and contemplation.

"There are many guests. There are many guests. Almost no one has time. Almost no one has time."

So goes the song, which aptly represents my daily routine in managing my material and spiritual health, for until today I haven't fully taken advantage of the abundant sunlight, food for the body, nor sought out daily silence, food for the soul.

Today, I decided to make a positive impact on my health: I began to spend a few minutes early in the morning and a few minutes late in the afternoon taking a sunbath for both body and soul.

Doctors agree that the sun is essential for the body and helps in the absorption of vitamin D.

Mystics agree that silence is a fundamental environment for allowing the Holy Spirit to work in our soul.

I installed an app on my phone to start, with three chimes, a period of a few minutes of silence, and to end with three chimes.

I sit comfortably in the sun and ask the Holy Spirit to relax my body, calm my mind, and soothe my heart.

I begin the minutes of silence, close my eyes, remain alert, in vigilance, feeling the present moment through the sensations experienced with my senses, touch and hearing, and mentally repeat the Christian mantra: Maranatha, an Aramaic phrase meaning 'Come, Lord.'

During this sunbath for the body and the soul, I strive to maintain 'a quiet mind, a straight spine, and a tranquil heart.'

How to keep within the Christian context

The Congregation for the Doctrine of the Faith published a Letter on Christian Meditation dated October 15, 1989,[33] which outlines the differences between Christian meditation and Hindu meditation.

The Christian faith holds that prayer is a gift from God. The Christian, even when alone, prays in union with the Divine Spirit that connects the Divine Son to the Divine Father.

Christian faith is monotheistic, while Hindu philosophy is pantheistic. The deep and intimate union of the person with God does not eliminate the separation between the Creator and the creature.

---

[33]

https://www.vatican.va/roman_curia/congregations/cfaith/documents/rc_con_cfaith_doc_19891015_meditazione-cristiana_po.html

In Christian meditation, one aspires to everything aspired to in other types of meditation, without the individual self of the creature disappearing into the ocean of God.

In Christian meditation, by receiving the Holy Spirit, that is, the love that unites the Divine Father and the Divine Son, the meditating person cries out, "Come, Lord," and thus, "The Holy Spirit itself joins our spirit to bear witness that we are children of God."[34]

Yes, we must 'empty' the spirit, but "so that a vacuum remains in the person praying that can then be 'filled' by divine richness. The vacuum that God needs is the renunciation of one's own selfishness, not necessarily the renunciation of the created things He has given us and among which He has placed us. There is no doubt that in prayer we should

____

[34] Romans 8,16

concentrate entirely on God and distance ourselves as much as possible from those things of this world that bind us to our selfishness. Saint Augustine is an eminent master on this point: if you want to find God — he says —, abandon the external world and enter yourself. However — he continues —, do not remain within yourself, but go beyond, because you are not God."

Your self is not God, but only a creature. God is 'interior intimo meo, et superior summo meo'. [35] God is within us and with us but transcends us.

The letter says: *"The Christian certainly needs specific times of retreat in solitude to gather and rediscover his way with God. But, given his status as a creature, and a creature who knows that all his security is in grace, his way of approaching God is not based on a*

---

[35] Saint Augustine, Confessions, 3, 6, 11

technique in the strict sense of the word. Such a fact would contradict the spirit of childhood required by the Gospel. Authentic Christian mysticism has nothing to do with technique: it is always a gift from God, of which the one who benefits feels unworthy."

The letter concludes:

"The love of God, the sole object of Christian contemplation, is a reality that we cannot 'possess' through any method or technique; on the contrary, we must always keep our gaze fixed on Jesus Christ, in Whom divine love on the cross reached such a point for us that He also took upon Himself the condition of being separated from the Father (Mark 15,34). Therefore, we must allow God to decide how He wants to make us participants in His love. But we can never, in any way, try to place ourselves on the same level as the object of contemplation, which is the free love of God. And this is even when, through the mercy of God the Father, by the Holy Spirit

sent to our hearts, we are given in Christ, freely, a sensible reflection of this divine love, and we feel ourselves drawn by the truth and beauty of the Lord. The more a creature is given to approach God, the more grows within it the reverential respect for the thrice-holy God. Thus, Saint Augustine's words are understood: 'You may call me friend, I recognize myself as a servant.'" [36]

---

[36] Saint Augustine, Expositions on the Psalms 142, 6

Science and Meditation

The book 'The Science of Meditation' by authors Daniel Goleman and Richard Davidson is not about meditation itself but about scientific research that studied the permanent changes in the brains of regular practitioners of meditation and yoga.

The research aimed to demystify or prove how regular meditation practice can permanently and positively change the way we think and feel.

Describing their extensive research work, the authors, who are both scientists and meditators, show how they sought to identify the effect of meditation on stress, genes, and attention, using tests and MRI and CT scans.

It is a scientific endorsement for a mystical practice.

About the Author

Décio Martins de Medeiros has published books on poetry, theology, religion, management, sales, genealogy, memoirs, and entertainment. He participates in the blog Prazer Compartilhar and the Clube de Autores.

Discover the covers and synopses of his books:
https://sites.google.com/view/autordeciomartins demedeiros/

Maranatha